NBA CHAMPIONSHIPS:

↓

2006, 2012, 2013

↓

ALL-TIME LEADING SCORER:

↓

DWYANE WADE (2003–16):

↓

20,221 POINTS

THE NBA: A HISTORY OF HOOPS

MIAMI HEAT

BY JIM WHITING

CREATIVE EDUCATION CREATIVE PAPERBACKS

Published by Creative Education
and Creative Paperbacks

P.O. Box 227, Mankato, Minnesota 56002
Creative Education and Creative Paperbacks
are imprints of The Creative Company
www.thecreativecompany.us

Design and production by Blue Design
Printed in the United States of America

Photographs by Alamy (Peter Phipp/Travelshots.
com), AP Images (ASSOCIATED PRESS), Corbis
(HANS DERYK/Reuters, Wang Lei/Xinhua Press),
Getty Images (Issac Baldizon/NBAE, Victor
Baldizon/NBAE, Andrew D. Bernstein/NBAE, Lou
Capozzola/NBAE, Angelo Cavalli, Rob Foldy/
Getty Images Sport, Jesse D. Garrabrant/NBAE,
Mike Lawrie/Getty Images Sport, Andy Lyons/
Allsport, John W. McDonough/Sports Illustrated,
Jim McIsaac/Getty Images Sport, Fernando
Medina/NBAE, Greg Nelson/Sports Illustrated,
Bob Rosato/Sports Illustrated, David Santiago/
El Nuevo Herald/TNS, Jamie Squire), Newscom
(FREDERIC J. BROWN/AFP/Getty Images, Robert
Duyos/MCT), USA Today Sports (Mark J. Rebilas)

Library of Congress Cataloging-in-Publication Data

Names: Whiting, Jim, 1943- author.

Title: Miami Heat / Jim Whiting.

Series: The NBA: A History of Hoops.

Includes bibliographical references and index.

Summary: This high-interest title summarizes
the history of the Miami Heat professional
basketball team, highlighting memorable events
and noteworthy players such as Dwyane Wade.

Identifiers: LCCN 2016054015 / ISBN 978-1-60818-
850-5 (hardcover) / ISBN 978-1-62832-453-2
(pbk) / ISBN 978-1-56660-898-5 (eBook)

Subjects: LCSH: 1. Miami Heat (Basketball team)—
History—Juvenile literature. 2. Miami Heat
(Basketball team)—Biography—Juvenile literature.

Classification: LCC GV885.52.M53 W45 2017 /
DDC 796.323/6409759381—dc23

CCSS: RI.4.1, 2, 3, 4; RI.5.1, 2, 4; RI.6.1, 2,
3; RF.4.3, 4; RF.5.3, 4; RH. 6-8. 4, 5, 7

First Edition HC 9 8 7 6 5 4 3 2 1

First Edition PBK 9 8 7 6 5 4 3 2 1

CONTENTS

LEGENDS OF THE HARDWOOD

8

The southernmost NBA city, MIAMI is known for sunny beaches and soaring temperatures.

THE HEAT START OUT COLD

The Miami Heat were in deep trouble. They had lost the first two games of the 2006 National Basketball Association (NBA) Finals to the Dallas Mavericks. In Game 3, they trailed by 14 points in the fourth quarter.

The 2006 Heat became the third team in NBA history to win the Finals after a 0–2 start.

A loss would almost certainly end their hopes. No team had ever come back from a 3–0 deficit. Heat guard Dwyane Wade didn't want to lose. With the clock winding down, he drained shot after shot. "(He) took over the game the last five, six minutes," said Heat center Shaquille O'Neal. Miami battled back to tie the score. Only a few seconds remained. With the game—and the season—on the line, the ball went to someone other than Wade. It was guard Gary Payton. He was a 16-year NBA veteran. Payton launched an 18-foot jumper. His basket won the game! He was modest about what he had done. "We've still got a lot of work to do," he said. "It's just fortunate that I made a shot and we won this game." Miami easily took the next matchup. Then it took a 3–2 lead with a one-point overtime win. Miami wrapped up the series with a 95–92 victory in Dallas. It was the Heat's first NBA title!

12

MIAMI'S FIRST PRO HOOPS TEAM

In 1968, the Minnesota Muskies of the American Basketball Association (ABA) moved to Miami. They changed their name to the Floridians. The team lasted four years. Three times they made the playoffs but never won a championship. One year, the Floridians played in Dinner Key Auditorium. The building was a former airplane hangar. It didn't have air conditioning. Sometimes it became very hot. The massive doors rumbled open. Ocean breezes whistled onto the court. Players had to adjust their shots for the breeze. Another year, the owner fired the entire team and started over. The Heat have worn replica Floridians jerseys a few times over the years.

By the mid-1980s, the NBA was rapidly increasing in popularity. Several cities wanted in on the action. Early in 1987, the NBA's expansion committee recommended adding North Carolina and Minnesota. They also suggested a third team be added in Florida. Both Miami and Orlando wanted the franchise. The two cities had long been commercial rivals. Now they began making media attacks on each other. The NBA moved quickly to defuse the problem. It said *both* cities would get teams. Officials of the new Miami team asked fans for name suggestions. Thousands responded. Barracudas, Beaches, Flamingos, Floridians, Palm Trees, Suntan, Shade, Sharks, and Tornadoes were just a few ideas. Several suggested Heat. "The Heat was it," said team official Zev Buffman. "When you think of Miami, that's what you think of."

When fans thought of Miami in the first season, they thought of losses. Lots of losses. The team set an NBA record by losing its first 17 games. Miami finally notched its first win on December 14. It defeated the Los Angeles Clippers, 89–88. But the Heat finished the season 15–67. It was the worst record in the NBA. Rookie Rony Seikaly was a bright spot. He established himself as one of the league's best centers. The Heat chose sharpshooting forward Glen Rice in the 1989 NBA Draft. But the team continued to struggle. Miami won just 18 games in 1989–90 and 24 the following season. Better days lay ahead. "The Heat have put together a nice group of kids," said Los Angeles Lakers coach Pat Riley. "If they give them some time to grow up, they'll have a good team."

HEATING UP

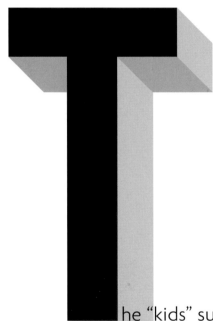

The "kids" surged to 38–44 in 1991–92. They qualified for the playoffs. But they faced the top-seeded Chicago Bulls. Miami lost every game. After the Heat failed to make the playoffs the following season, Rice challenged his teammates. "We're not kids

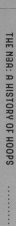

THE NBA: A HISTORY OF HOOPS

17

Intimidating center **ALONZO MOURNING** often followed his blocks with a battle cry.

anymore," he said. "The fans have been patient with us. Now it's time to reward them."

The Heat listened to Rice. They finished 42–40 in 1993–94. It was the team's first winning record. Miami faced the top-seeded Atlanta Hawks in the playoffs. The Heat took a 2–1 lead before Atlanta rallied. The Hawks ended Miami's season. The Heat couldn't maintain the momentum. They dropped to 32 wins the following season. Team officials made a key move before the 1995–96 season. They hired Riley as coach. He already had four NBA titles to his credit. "We're going to build this franchise into a winner the only way I know how," he said. "We're going to bring in the best players, and we'll work harder than anyone else." He reshaped the roster, bringing in players such as All-Star center Alonzo Mourning and lightning-quick point guard Tim Hardaway. Miami won 42 games and faced Chicago in the playoffs. The Bulls had won an NBA record 72 games.

THE ULTIMATE INSULT

For many years, Miami was the most important city in Florida. But in 1971, Walt Disney World opened in Orlando. The two cities began competing for tourist dollars. The situation grew worse when they competed for an NBA franchise. Patrick Williams, a representative for Orlando's bid, frequently pointed out Miami's reputation for crime. "When I approached the checkout counter of a Miami store," he joked, "the sales clerk said, 'Cash, charge, or stickup?'" Miami fought back. "We don't have Mickey Mouse here," said city manager Cesar Odio, "but then, we're not a Mickey Mouse city, either." The ultimate insult came when a Miami newspaper called Mickey Mouse a rat. Awarding franchises to both cities helped end that battle.

Forward **DAN MAJERLE** and the Heat fell to the Bulls in the 1997 conference finals.

Chicago won all 3 games, by an average of 23 points.

Riley continued to tinker with the roster. He put emphasis on playing solid defense. The result was a surprising 61–21 season. Riley was named Coach of the Year. This time, there would be no early playoff exit. Miami won the first two rounds. It faced Chicago in the Eastern Conference finals. Once again, the Bulls had too much firepower. Miami won just one game.

he Heat continued to perform well. They won 55 games in 1997–98, 33 in the strike-shortened 1998–99 season, and 52 the following season. They also had a new nemesis: the New York Knicks. The Heat had defeated the Knicks in the 1997 playoffs. The Knicks returned the favor in 1998. They defeated the Heat, three games to two. The same thing happened the following season. That series was especially disheartening. Miami was the top seed. It lost the deciding Game 5 by a single point on a jump shot with less than a second

22

The Heat and the Knicks engaged in fierce competition during the 1990s.

remaining on the clock. "Life in basketball has a lot of suffering in it," Riley said. "And we will suffer this one."

The suffering at the hands of the Knicks continued the following season. This time, the teams met in the second round. Late in the final game, New York's Patrick Ewing dunked the ball for an 83–82 lead. Again, the Heat lost by a single point. The four-year rivalry was intense. It was packed with fights and close games. "It might not have been the most artistic, but from an effort standpoint, from a defensive standpoint, from a competitive standpoint, ... it was some of the best basketball that's ever been played," Riley said.

CRAZY EIGHTS

CHICAGO BULLS AT MIAMI HEAT, FEBRUARY 23, 1996

The Heat had just made a blockbuster trade. Tim Hardaway and four other players were on their way to Miami. But they didn't arrive in time to play against the Bulls. "It was a throwaway game to me," said coach Pat Riley. "We had eight guys. We had to hustle guard Tony Smith in here quick just to be legal." The Heat lived up to their name. Guard Rex Chapman was almost glowing. He sank 9 of 10 field goals. He finished with a career-high 39 points. "Rex just had one of those nights," Riley said. Miami won, 113–104. It was 1 of just 10 Bulls losses that year.

24

DRAFTING DWYANE

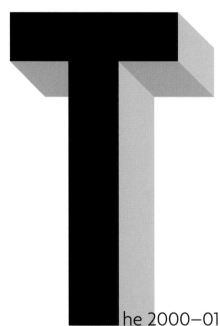

The 2000–01 season began with bad news. Mourning had a rare kidney disease. He missed most of the season. His teammates wanted to pick up the slack. "Alonzo is our leader, but this is an

High-scoring TIM HARDAWAY brought flashy style and ball-handling to Miami.

At 7-foot-1 and 325 pounds, All-Star SHAQUILLE O'NEAL was a force at the basket.

> "ALONZO IS OUR LEADER, BUT THIS IS AN OPPORTUNITY FOR THE REST OF US TO LEAD IN HIS ABSENCE," SAID FORWARD DAN MAJERLE. "WE WON'T QUIT, BECAUSE WE OWE THAT TO ZO."

opportunity for the rest of us to lead in his absence," said forward Dan Majerle. "We won't quit, because we owe that to Zo." Miami went on to win 50 games that season. But the Charlotte Hornets swept the Heat in the first round of the playoffs. Miami slumped to 36 wins the following season. It was the first time in Riley's 20-year head coaching career that his team didn't make the playoffs. The Heat did even worse in 2002–03. They won only 25 games. Mourning left the team in free agency. Riley stepped down as coach. Assistant coach Stan Van Gundy took over the next season. Riley remained with the team as general manager.

Miami drafted shooting guard Dwyane Wade with the fifth overall selection of the 2003 NBA Draft. The Heat improved to 42 wins in his rookie year. Wade averaged more than 16 points a game. He was third in line for Rookie of the Year. Only superstars LeBron James and Carmelo Anthony were ahead of him. The Heat beat the New Orleans Hornets in the first round of the playoffs. But they couldn't get past the Indiana Pacers in the second round. The Pacers won the series, 4–2. Miami made a monster trade for O'Neal after the season. "Today, the Miami Heat took a giant step forward in our continued pursuit of an NBA championship for the city of Miami and this franchise," Riley said.

The trade paid off. With Shaq dominating the middle, Miami surged to a 59–23 mark. The Heat swept their opponents in the first two rounds of the playoffs. Then they faced the Detroit Pistons in the Eastern

Coach **PAT RILEY** brought star players to Miami and turned the Heat into a powerhouse.

Conference finals. Miami took a 3–2 edge. But Wade suffered a painful rib injury near the end of the fifth game. He had to watch Game 6 in street clothes. The Pistons drubbed the Heat, 91–66. "Obviously, not having him [Wade], that impacted the game so much," said Pistons coach Larry Brown. "You know, Dwyane … makes everybody better. Dwyane has the same effect on the game at both ends. Obviously it helped." Wade returned for Game 7 but had to play hurt. "He didn't have his explosiveness," said teammate Keyon Dooling. "He was in a lot of pain." Detroit took the series with an 88–82 Game 7 win.

LEGENDS OF THE HARDWOOD

SCHOOL OF HARD KNOCKS

DWYANE WADE, SHOOTING GUARD, 6-FOOT-4, 2003–2016

Dwyane Wade had a tough childhood. His parents were divorced. His mother was a drug addict. He lived in a rough neighborhood in Chicago. Wade's father didn't want his son to join the gang culture. They played basketball for hours on end. "He taught me the game, what I needed to know to win games," Wade said. "My toughness on the court came from him knocking me down and not picking me up.... He was one of the biggest influences on me." His father laid down rules. No tattoos. No earrings. No baseball caps. Today, Wade encourages young people to follow similar rules. He supports numerous charities in Chicago and Miami.

O'NEAL grabbed 10.2 rebounds per game in the 2006 Finals.

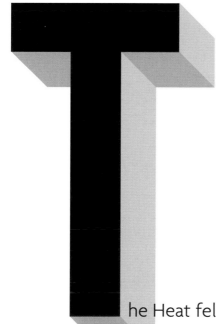

TAKING THE TITLE

The Heat fell off a little in the 2005–06 regular season. They won 52 games. Again they faced Detroit in the conference finals. This time, though, the outcome was different. Miami won the series, 4–2.

Guard **JASON WILLIAMS** helped the Heat take the title with his thrilling passes and assists.

32

Now it took on the Dallas Mavericks for the NBA title. Payton's clutch shot gave Miami the Game 3 win. Wade had a career-high 42 points. He added 13 rebounds. Wade kept his foot on the gas in the next three games. He scored 36 points, then 43, then 36 again. Miami won all three games to secure the NBA championship. It was only the third team in NBA history to win the title after losing the first two games. Wade was an obvious choice for Finals Most Valuable Player (MVP). "I didn't have the best game," said O'Neal. "But D-Wade's been doing it all year. He's the best player ever."

Heat fans hoped for a repeat title the following season. But Wade suffered a severe shoulder injury and missed nearly half the season. Miami won 44 games. Chicago swept the Heat in the first round of the playoffs. Wade missed much of the 2007–08 season with

34

FROM HOSPITAL TO HARDWOOD

DETROIT PISTONS AT MIAMI HEAT, 2006 NBA EASTERN CONFERENCE FINALS, GAME 6, JUNE 2, 2006

Dwyane Wade was brilliant in the first five games of the series. He averaged more than 29 points a game. But Wade got sick before Game 6. "At 3 A.M. is really when I woke up and I knew I wasn't going to go back to sleep," he said. "The trainer told me I needed to get to the hospital. I stayed at the hospital until 3 P.M. Then I went home and changed and came to the game." Wade started slowly. He spent extra time in the locker room at halftime taking fluids. Somehow, he played 37 minutes. He scored 14 points and dished out 10 assists. Miami won. The Heat went on to become the NBA champions.

a knee injury. O'Neal was traded midseason. Miami won just 15 games. That matched the franchise's worst record. Wade was fully healthy the following season. He led the league in scoring with an average of 30.2 points per game. The Heat's two draft choices, forward Michael Beasley and point guard Mario Chalmers, made important contributions. Miami improved to 43–39. It lost to Atlanta in the first round of the playoffs, 4–3. The Heat won 47 games the following season. Again they made an early playoff exit, falling to the Boston Celtics, 4–1.

ade became a free agent after the season. Miami wanted him to stay. The Chicago Bulls wanted him to come home and play for them. It was a tough decision. He asked family members to vote. It was a tie. The tiebreaker came from power forward Chris Bosh. The Toronto Raptors had drafted him in 2003.

"STEADY" EDDIE JONES brought consistent guarding to Miami for five seasons.

"YOU HAVE THREE GUYS, ALL-STARS, IN THE PRIME OF THEIR CAREER," SAID ORLANDO MAGIC COACH STAN VAN GUNDY. "THAT'S A HECKUVA TEAM TO MATCH UP AGAINST."

That was the same year Miami took Wade. Bosh established numerous records with the Raptors. Now he was also a free agent. He announced that he was moving south to play for Miami. Wade immediately said he would stay. There was one more prize free agent from the 2003 Draft. That was LeBron James. He had become a superstar with the Cleveland Cavaliers. Less than 48 hours after Bosh's announcement, James signed with Miami. "You have three guys, All-Stars, in the prime of their career," said Orlando Magic coach Stan Van Gundy. "That's a heckuva team to match up against."

38

THE "BIG THREE" ERA

most teams had trouble matching up with the "Big Three" and their teammates. The Heat won 58 games. They easily won the Eastern Conference title.

CHRIS BOSH and his superstar teammates formed a Miami juggernaut.

40

BEST GAME ... EVER?

SAN ANTONIO SPURS AT MIAMI HEAT, GAME 6, NBA FINALS, JUNE 18, 2013

The San Antonio Spurs seemed ready to close out the series. They led by 5 points with 28 seconds left. League officials acted like the game was over. They brought out yellow tape to keep spectators off the floor. Then LeBron James sank a three-point shot. San Antonio scored a free throw. With less than 10 seconds to go, Ray Allen drained a field goal to send the game into overtime. Allen's two free throws with two seconds left in overtime gave Miami a 103–100 win. "It was by far the best game that I've ever been a part of," James said.

LeBRON JAMES led Miami to back-to-back NBA championships in 2012 and 2013.

But the Mavericks defeated Miami in the NBA Finals, 4–2. A strike shortened the 2011–12 season. James was named the league's MVP as the Heat won 46 games. They dominated the Oklahoma City Thunder in the NBA Finals, 4–1. "Winning a championship, it's the reason that we all came here together," Wade said. "And I'm not just talking about Chris, LeBron, and myself…. I'm talking about all these guys." Miami added veteran three-point specialist Ray Allen and had its best year ever in 2012–13. The Heat won 66 games. That included a 27-game winning streak. It was the second-longest single-

Miami's "Big Three" combined for nearly 70 points per game in 2011–12.

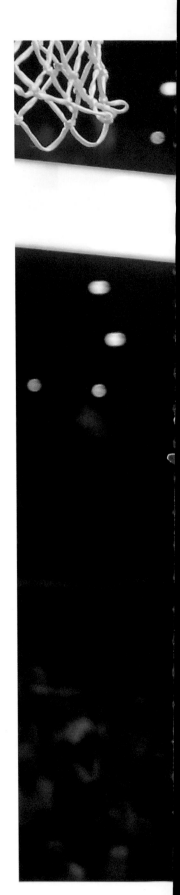

season streak in NBA history! James repeated as MVP. The Heat came back from a 3–2 deficit in the NBA Finals to defeat the San Antonio Spurs and win their second straight title.

Heat fans felt confident that the team would "three-peat" in the following season. Once again, the Heat dominated the regular season with 54 wins. And again, they faced the Spurs for the championship. With the series tied at a game apiece, the Heat fell apart. The Spurs won 3 straight games by an average of 19 points. James jilted Miami

Point guard **GORAN DRAGIC** led the Heat back to the postseason in 2015–16.

Towering center HASSAN WHITESIDE led the league in blocked shots in 2015–16.

soon afterward. He returned to Cleveland. The Heat added two-time All-Star small forward Luol Deng and center Hassan Whiteside to try to make up for losing James. But Bosh suffered a leg injury early in the season. Then he missed several months with a blood clot in his lung. The Heat stumbled to a 37–45 mark. They rebounded the following season to win 48 games. Miami lost to the Toronto Raptors in the second round of the playoffs. The Heat struggled for much of the 2016–17 season. But they didn't give up. Miami finished with a rush, going 17–9 to end with a 41–41 mark. It missed the playoffs by a single game. A basket here, a free throw there could have led to a matchup with Eastern Conference champion Boston.

In their short history, the Miami Heat have become an important part of life in South Florida. Three titles in eight seasons gave fans a thirst for more. The team's continuing star power certainly makes that a realistic expectation.

SELECTED BIBLIOGRAPHY

Ballard, Chris. *The Art of a Beautiful Game: The Thinking Fan's Tour of the NBA*. New York: Simon & Schuster, 2010.

Hareas, John. *Ultimate Basketball: More Than 100 Years of the Sport's Evolution*. New York: DK, 2004.

Hubbard, Jan, ed. *The Official NBA Basketball Encyclopedia*. 3rd edition. New York: Doubleday, 2000.

NBA.com. "Miami Heat." http://www.nba.com/heat/.

Simmons, Bill. *The Book of Basketball: The NBA According to the Sports Guy*. New York: Ballantine, 2009.

Sports Illustrated. *Sports Illustrated Basketball's Greatest*. New York: Sports Illustrated, 2014.

WEBSITES

HEAT YOUTH BASKETBALL

http://www.nba.com/heat/community/youth_basketball.html/

Learn more about the Heat's involvement with youth, including their basketball clinics.

JR. NBA

http://jr.nba.com/

This kids site has games, videos, game results, team and player information, statistics, and more.

Note: Every effort has been made to ensure that any websites listed above were active at the time of publication. However, because of the nature of the Internet, it is impossible to guarantee that these sites will remain active indefinitely or that their contents will not be altered.

47

INDEX